IRISH FAMILY FOOD

Irish Family Food

RUTH ISABEL ROSS

Gill & Macmillan

Gill & Macmillan Ltd
Goldenbridge
Dublin 8
with associated companies throughout the world
© Ruth Isabel Ross 1996

0 7171 2405 3
Editorial Consultant: Roberta Reeners
Illustrations by Tom Brady
Design and print origination by
Identikit Design Consultants, Dublin
Index compiled by Helen Litton
Printed by The Guernsey Press Ltd

A catalogue record is available for this book
from the British Library.

1 3 5 4 2

Table of Contents

INTRODUCTION

CONVERSION TABLE   xi

Irish Breakfasts

Porridge	2
Traditional Breakfast Fry	3

Soups

Potato Soup	5
Lentil Soup	6
Chicken Broth	7
Deep Sea Soup	8
Mulligatawny Soup	9
Gamekeeper Soup	10
Scotch Broth	11

Fish Dishes

Fish Cakes	13
Family Fish Pie	14
Special Fish Pie	15
Fried Herrings in Oatmeal	16
Grilled Mackerel	17
Baked Salmon	18

The Meat Course

Boiled Corned Beef with Carrots
and Dumplings   21
Chicken Pot Roast   22
Irish Stew   23
Lancashire Hotpot   24
Roast Duck with Sage Stuffing   25
Steak and Kidney Pudding   26
Toad-in-the-Hole   27
Stuffed Fillets of Pork   29
Roast Beef   29
Cottage Pie   31
Braised Beef in Guinness   32
Brown Stew with Guinness   33
Roast Lamb with Rosemary   34
Dublin Coddle   35
Bacon and Cabbage   36

Ways with Potatoes

Champ   38
Colcannon   39
Bubble-and-Squeak   40
Potato Cakes   41

Extras

Roast Meat Gravy 43
Forcemeat Balls 43
Roast Savoury Dumplings 44
Simmered Dumplings 45
Potato Stuffing 46
Yorkshire Pudding 46
Cheese Fingers 48
Tomatoes in Vinaigrette Dressing 49
Herb Butter 51

Pastry

Suet Crust 53
Rich Shortcrust Pastry 54
Rough Puff Pastry 55

Hot Puddings

Apple Amber 57
Apple Dumpling 58
Bread-and-Butter Pudding 59
Rice Pudding 60
Steamed Sponge 61
Treacle Tart 62
Roly-Poly Pudding 63
Spicy Baked Apples 64
Pancakes 65

Cold Puddings

Gooseberry Fool	68
Summer Pudding	69
Sillabub	70
Blackberry Ice Cream	71

Preserves and Jams

Lemon Curd	74
Strawberry Jam	75
Almack's Preserve	76
Marrow, Ginger and Whiskey Jam	77
Mint Jelly	78
Gooseberry Jelly with Elderflowers	79
Light Blackcurrant Jam	80
Thin Marmalade	81
Green Tomato Chutney	82

Sauces

Apple Sauce	84
Mint Sauce	85
Horseradish Sauce	86
Parsley Sauce	87
Thick White Sauce	88
INDEX	89

Introduction

F amily food in Ireland was planned to console, to warm and to satisfy.

After working long hours in windy fields or trudging home from school, what could make a family happier than to tuck into a large plateful of hot Irish stew, straight from the saucepan? On fast days, and these used to be every Friday, there would be large fish pies or creamed potatoes, made savoury with chopped onion and melting butter. These would be followed by either a hot pudding or freshly-made bread spread thickly with yellow farm butter and homemade jam.

This food, with local variations, was wholesome, nourishing and plain, just tasting of itself. Only on very special occasions was it ever indulgent. Ingredients were fresh and cooking was slow and gentle, bringing out every flavour.

Many years ago, Irish stew, bacon and cabbage, colcannon and other national favourites were enhanced by dishes from Scotland and other regions of Britain. Scotch broth, Lancashire hotpot and Yorkshire pudding became part of family fare — so much so that if it weren't for their names, no one would know that these and other popular standbys did not originate in Ireland.

Times have changed. Mornings are so rushed these days that we do without fried breakfasts. Houses are warmer, making salads more attractive. We have been abroad and taken to pasta and scampi, and we now enjoy exciting fruit and vegetables from all over the world. All of this is healthy and outward looking.

But first love never quite goes away. Traditional food is as much a part of our culture as the Hill of Tara. It gives us a secure back-to-the-womb feeling. Carefully cooked, it helps to keep family life alive and well.

Conversion Table

Imperial	US	International (Metric)
1 tsp	1¼ tsp	6 ml
1 tbsp = 3 tsp	1¼ tbsp	18 ml
1 cup = 10 oz	1¼ cups = 10 oz	296 ml
1 pt = 2 cups, 20 oz	1¼ pt = 2½ cups, 20 oz	591 ml

US	Imperial	International (Metric)
1 tsp	¾ tsp	5 ml
1 tbsp = 3 tsp	¾ tbsp	15 ml
1 cup = 8 oz	¾ cup	237 ml (approx ¼ l)
1 pt = 2 cups, 16 oz	⅘ pt = 1⅔ cups, 16 oz	473 ml (approx ½ l)

Irish Breakfasts

Porridge
Traditional Breakfast Fry

'Irish breakfasts are not what they used to be,' some
people complain, thinking back longingly to plates piled
with slices of bacon, sausages, black pudding, white pudding,
tomatoes, eggs and potato cakes — not to mention plenty of
fried bread.

Certainly the rush of modern life and the worry about
cholesterol have caused the collapse of the universal Irish
breakfast. All the same, this hearty meal is still consumed by
farmers and farm workers, by people who stay in bed-and-
breakfast accommodation, and by train commuters between
places like Dublin and Cork. And many more people who
scuttle to work all week on half a piece of toast and a gulp of
tea revel in an Irish breakfast at the weekends.

There are two constituents to an Irish breakfast, porridge
and 'a fry'. People do not usually have both any more.

Porridge

We are told that porridge is positively good for us. So it is worth
persevering with this acquired taste, especially if we have a
non-stick saucepan, as porridge sticks stubbornly onto saucepans.
Buy quick-cooking oats and follow the instructions on the packet.
They will probably be something like this.

'Boil 3 teacupsful of water in a saucepan. Empty 1 teacupful of quick-cooking oats into the boiling water. Bring it to the boil again, stirring all the time.'

Let the mixture simmer for as long as the instructions advise, probably about 10 minutes. Continue stirring. It will thicken.

Serve immediately with brown sugar and fresh milk or cream.

Some people, often Scots, like salt with their porridge.

If you have a continuous-burning kitchen stove, you can make the porridge the previous night and leave it in a warm place. We do this ourselves — it saves time in the morning and makes enough for 2 generous servings.

Traditional Breakfast Fry

Everyone has his or her own way of frying or, with the more health conscious, grilling/broiling for breakfast. It is better not to be in a hurry. This is why a cooked breakfast tastes so good on a leisurely weekend morning, turning naturally into a brunch.

These are well-known instructions for bacon, eggs and fried bread. They can be enhanced by sausages, tomatoes, sliced white or black pudding* and mushrooms, while the bacon and eggs wait in a warm oven. The eggs may also be held over and cooked last. Bacon is always the first thing to be put in the pan as it gives that special flavour to everything else.

For each person you need:
3 thinly-cut rashers (slices) of bacon
1 or 2 eggs
1 slice bread

Put the bacon in an oiled and buttered frying pan and heat it slowly. Fry until crisp — there should be hot fat in the frying pan at this point. Place the bacon onto the bread (it will absorb the bacon juices). Keep warm.

Fry the eggs one by one in the hot bacon fat, basting them thoroughly — you may need a little more oil or butter.

Fry the bread lightly and put it back under the rashers. Put everything onto warm plates. Serve at once.

*Black pudding and white pudding are vaguely similar to German wursts. However, they contain more grain or meal and are not as fatty or juicy.

Soups

꙰

Potato Soup
Lentil Soup
Chicken Broth
Deep Sea Soup
Mulligatawny Soup
Gamekeeper Soup
Scotch Broth

S oups in Ireland are thick and nourishing. They restore us after a cold day outside or at the end of a long journey. The goodness runs down to our toes without tiring the digestion.

Some of the following soups are simple — potato soup, lentil soup and Scotch broth, for instance. Others, like Mulligatawny, gamekeeper and deep sea soups, are more sophisticated. They are all full of good things and can be liquidised or not, as you like.

Many of these soups can make meals in themselves, and as such are recommended by doctors as the healthiest form of nourishment after a long aeroplane flight.

It seems almost wicked to write about soups without recommending that cooks make their own stock. In the old days, stock was always the basis of soups. However, it is tedious to make and clutters up the kitchen and the saucepans. Excellent soups prepared with fresh ingredients need no stock at all. A compromise is to save carrot or bean water for a few days and to simmer any chicken carcass for 6 hours. This will give an adequate stock.

Potato Soup

This is a popular standby. It can be made partly with stock from boiled bacon or boiled corned beef water, although not entirely as the taste might be too strong. Traditionally, we make potato soup with leeks or onions and add whatever herbs we have to hand.

Serves 2.

25 g/1 oz/2 US tbsp butter or margarine
225 g/½ lb potatoes, diced
1 onion or leek, diced
600 ml/1 pint/2½ cups water or stock
thyme and parsley, chopped
salt and pepper

Melt the butter gently in a saucepan. Dice the potatoes and leek and sweat them in the butter for 5 minutes. Do not let them brown.

Add the water or stock, half the herbs and the seasoning. Simmer it all slowly. When the vegetables are soft and the soup thickened by the potato, throw in the rest of the chopped herbs. Liquidise and serve very hot with croûtons of fried bread.

Lentil Soup

Boiled corned beef stock (page 21) is often used for
this heart-warming soup. If the soup is too salty,
dilute it with a little water.
Serves 4.

3 dsp/4½ US tbsp lentils
1 large potato, diced
2 carrots, sliced
1 dsp/1½ US tbsp chives and thyme, chopped
900 ml/1½ pints/3¾ cups stock
50 g/2 oz/½ cup peas (fresh or frozen)

Simmer the lentils, potato, carrots and half the herbs in the stock until tender.

Add the peas and the rest of the herbs. Cook for 15 minutes. Liquidise and return to the saucepan.

Reheat and serve with dark brown bread.

Chicken Broth

A simple version of this family soup.
Serves 4.

1.2 L/2 pints/5 cups chicken stock
2 leeks, diced
2 large carrots, diced
6 sticks celery, diced
¼ head of cabbage, shredded
thyme, sage and parsley
2 slices bread roll per person

Dice all the vegetables except the cabbage, which should be shredded. Simmer them, with half the herbs, in the stock for ¾ hour or longer. They should integrate and the stock should reduce. Test for seasoning.

Brown the slices of roll slightly and put two into each heated soup plate/bowl.

Lift out the vegetables with a slotted spoon and cover the bread slices with them.

Add the remaining herbs to the stock and pour it over each helping.

Deep Sea Soup

Derived distantly from Bouillabaisse.
Serves 4.

4 medium-sized potatoes, floury* and dry
6 spring onions, chopped
2 tomatoes, peeled (optional)
125 g/¼ lb runner (green) beans, chopped (optional)
25 g/1 oz/¼ stick margarine or butter
1.2 L/2 pints/5 cups water
thyme and parsley, chopped
350 g/12 oz/¾ lb thick cod, filleted and skinned
125 g/¼ lb shelled prawns (or other shellfish)

C hop the potatoes roughly and cook gently in butter with the onions, tomatoes and beans for about 5 minutes.

Add water and half the chopped herbs. Simmer gently until the potatoes have disintegrated.

Cut prepared cod into bite-sized squares. Add to the soup, along with the prawns. Poach gently. This will take only a few minutes.

Add the rest of the herbs and test for seasoning. Ladle into soup plates/bowls.

With crisp French bread, this makes a delicious Sunday night supper. Less liquid and more fish gives us a nourishing fish stew.

*A mature russet-type potato is best as it is
fluffier ('floury') and less moist.*

Mulligatawny Soup

Enjoyed especially by those who have lived in India.
Serves 4.

1 onion, chopped
1 cooking apple, chopped
25 g/1 oz/¼ stick butter or margarine
1 tbsp/1¼ US tbsp mild curry powder
1.2 L/2 pints/5 cups water
1 small potato, chopped (for thickening)
1 tbsp/1¼ US tbsp mango chutney

Chop the onion and apple. Cook in butter or margarine until golden brown.

Mix the curry powder with a little cold water and add this to the onion and apple mixture. Cook gently for a few minutes.

Add the water, chopped potato and chutney. Simmer for ½ hour.

Liquidise, then reheat.

Serve with a bowl of fluffy white rice.

Gamekeeper Soup

*This is the best soup of all in mid-winter. It can be made
from any game bird, although pheasant is the nicest.
Add more red wine if the weather is very cold.*

Serves 4.

2 pheasant carcasses

leftover meat of ½ pheasant, diced (about 1 teacup)

thyme and sage, to taste

salt and pepper, to taste

2 leeks, chopped

2 large carrots, chopped

½ head celery, chopped

4 oz/½ cup dry red wine

1 tbsp/1¼ US tbsp redcurrant or bramble jelly

B reak up the pheasant bones roughly and put them in a
saucepan with enough water to cover. Add half the
meat and half the herbs. Season.

Simmer slowly for 6 hours at least. Let the stock
reduce a little to about 1½ pints.

Pour the stock into a jug to cool. When it is cold, skim
any fat off the surface.

Put the chopped vegetables into the skimmed stock and
simmer gently for 1 hour. (The vegetables will absorb the
gamey flavour.) Stir in the jelly and the remaining herbs.

Add the rest of the meat and the wine. Reheat and
serve at once.

Scotch Broth

With more meat and vegetables and with less liquid,
this soup becomes a satisfying stew.
Serves 4.

350 g/12 oz lamb gigot (chop)
1 tbsp/1¼ US tbsp pearl barley
1 carrot, diced
1 onion, diced
50 g/2 oz/½ cup peas (fresh or frozen)
salt and pepper, to taste
2 tbsp/2½ US tbsp parsley, chopped

Cut the meat into small pieces. Put any pieces of bone into a little boiling water to help make a stock.

Make the stock up to 600 ml/1 pint/2½ cups by adding more water.

Put the meat and barley into the stock. Bring slowly to the boil. Skim off any froth and simmer the mixture slowly for 2 hours. About 20 minutes before serving, add the vegetables, along with salt and pepper.

Add chopped parsley just before serving piping hot.

Fish Dishes

Fish Cakes
Family Fish Pie
Special Fish Pie
Fried Herrings in Oatmeal
Grilled Mackerel
Baked Salmon

I rish people have mixed feelings about fish. It was often eaten on most Fridays, but as part of a fast day. This meant that fish was considered rather a second-class food. Also, it was hard to buy fresh fish in the midland counties of Ireland. All of this put people off.

Since the fast day has disappeared and transport has improved, fish has become more popular. Some of it is much sought after. A good fish shop will now stock monkfish, mussels and fresh prawns, as well as the inevitable cod and haddock.

Families still like the old ways of cooking fish, especially in savoury fish cakes or creamy fish pies. They also like the strong taste of herring or mackerel.

Fish Cakes

An economical meal. A small amount of fish goes a long way
in fish cakes which are popular with children.
Serves 2.

225 g/½ lb potatoes, mashed
125 g/4 oz/½ cup fish, cooked and flaked (white fish, salmon
or trout, or a mixture)
1 dsp/1½ US tbsp parsley, chopped
salt to taste
25 g /1 oz/¼ stick butter, melted
1 egg yolk
flour
to fry: butter, oil and bacon fat

M ix the mashed potato and flaked fish in a bowl. Add
the parsley, salt, melted butter and egg yolk.

With floured hands, form 6 balls from the mixture.
Flatten them down and coat with more flour.

Fry in shallow fat made from butter, oil and bacon
fat, if you have it. The fish cakes will quickly become
golden-brown, top and bottom. They can then be put in a
brisk oven for a few minutes to help them become piping hot.

Serve with lemon wedges and tartar sauce.

Fish cakes can also be finished with egg and
breadcrumbs and deep-fat fried.

Family Fish Pie

*Lovely when made with salmon or trout, it can also be made
with white or smoked fish or a mixture of both. A little fish
goes a long way in such an economical recipe.*

Serves 4.

450 g/1 lb potatoes, boiled and mashed
25 g/1 oz/¼ stick butter
280 ml/½ pint/1¼ cups hot milk (approximately)
salt to taste
350 g/12 oz/1½ cups poached fish, flaked
1 tbsp/1½ US tbsp parsley, chopped
2 hard-boiled eggs (optional)

FOR SAUCE

(page 88)
25 g/1 oz/¼ stick butter
25 g/1 oz/2 US tbsp plain (all-purpose) flour
280 ml/½ pint/1¼ cups milk

Put the potatoes on to simmer while you make the sauce. When the sauce has thickened and is properly cooked, pour it onto the flaked fish, parsley and egg mixture. Transfer it all into a shallow casserole dish. Keep warm.

Mash the cooked potatoes thoroughly and heat them with the butter and hot milk. They must be really creamy. Taste in case they need more salt. Spread the creamed potatoes over the fish mixture. Put slivers of butter on top.

Bake at 220°C/425°F/gas 7 for 30 minutes. If the crust is not a nice, crisp golden-brown, push it under a grill/broiler for a few minutes.

Serve at once.

Special Fish Pie

*Sheila, a vigorous friend, used to cook this fish pie
as a treat for her three sons.*

Serves 4.

350 g/12 oz rough puff pastry (page 55)
thick white sauce (page 88)
350 g/12 oz/1½ cups white fish, cooked and flaked
pepper and salt
parsley, chopped
milk and egg, to brush

Roll the pastry into a square.

Mix the fish into the white sauce, adding pepper and salt to taste. Let it cool a little. Put the fish mixture into the pastry square. Sprinkle with parsley.

Bring up the corners of pastry to meet in the middle. It should look like an envelope. Brush milk on the seams to make them stick together. Brush the whole top with milk or egg. Place on a baking sheet and bake at 200°C/400°F/gas 6 for 10 minutes. Then cover the pie with foil and lower the temperature to 190°C/375°F/gas 5. Continue baking for a further 30-35 minutes.

Fried Herrings in Oatmeal

A popular and economical fish in winter.
As children have difficulty with bones, it is not
suitable for the very young.
The herrings should be gutted, trimmed and
the heads cut off.

1 small herring per person
oatmeal (or flour) to coat
butter
1 dsp/1½ US tbsp olive oil

Coat the herrings with oatmeal or flour.
Melt the butter and oil in a frying pan.

When the fat is really hot, put in the coated herrings and fry briskly on each side for 5-7 minutes. The skin should become brown and crisp.

Serve at once, very hot, with lemon wedges.

Herrings can also be roasted in the oven.

Grilled Mackerel

Mackerel is a popular fish in Irish coastal towns. It needs to be extra fresh and tastes better eaten on the bone, although children find fillets much easier to handle. Either way, mackerel is succulent when grilled/broiled.

1 small fish or fillet per person
olive oil to brush over
lemon slices
herb butter (page 51)

Preheat the grill/broiler.

If cooking the whole fish, make 3 deep incisions on each side. Brush the skins well with olive oil. Put the fish under the hot grill/broiler. With fillets, start with the skin side uppermost.

Brush again with oil before turning. Brush the top side and continue grilling/broiling. The fish should be ready after 15 minutes in all.

Serve immediately with slices of lemon and herb butter (page 51).

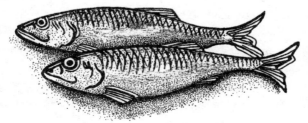

Baked Salmon

Irish salmon was the greatest summer treat, more for grown-ups
than for children. The tail-end is the more economical
piece and tastes good when cooked quite simply.
Salmon trout is cooked the same way. The fish should be gutted
and trimmed, and washed under a running tap/faucet.
Serves 4.

1 × 1.35 kg/3 lb tail-end of salmon
or
1 × 1.35 kg/3 lb salmon trout (head removed, if you prefer)
50 g/2 oz/½ stick butter
juice of ½ lemon
1 tbsp/1¼ US tbsp mixed herbs (chives, parsley and
marjoram are most suitable)
salt

Lay the fish on a large, well-buttered sheet of tinfoil. Sprinkle with the lemon juice, herbs and a little salt. Fold over the tinfoil.

Bake in the oven at 180°C/350°F/gas 4 for about 30 minutes. Test for cooking with a carving fork.

If you are eating it hot, remove the skin and transfer the fish to a warm plate. Pour the juices over it. Put some slabs of herb butter (page 51) on the surface to melt. See that it comes to the table very warm. Serve with new potatoes and courgettes/zucchini or peas.

If you want to eat it cold, leave the fish to cool in its skin (this keeps it moist). Cold salmon and salmon trout are usually eaten with cucumber.

The Meat Course

Boiled Corned Beef with Carrots and Dumplings
Chicken Pot Roast
Irish Stew
Lancashire Hotpot
Roast Duck with Sage Stuffing
Steak and Kidney Pudding
Toad-in-the-Hole
Stuffed Fillets of Pork
Roast Beef
Cottage Pie
Braised Beef in Guinness
Brown Stew with Guinness
Roast Lamb with Rosemary
Dublin Coddle
Bacon and Cabbage

M eat was thought essential for health in the old days, though helpings were often frugal and there was little frying of wasteful steaks or chops. Mostly the food was simple, like toad-in-the-hole, Irish stew and cottage pie, but occasionally there was game or duck, and very good it was.

Cruel factory farming, which keeps chickens and pigs immobile for their whole lives, has made pork and chicken cheaper. It is worth paying the higher price, if you can, for better-flavoured, free-range chicken and pork to encourage brave organic farmers. Beef and lamb are still reared healthily here on green pastures.

There were many mixtures to accompany meat — savoury stuffings for birds, forcemeat balls to slide into the roasting pan, dumplings for stew. And there were the well-known pastry and suet crusts for meat pies and puddings.

Did these dishes take long to prepare? They were started early, certainly, but then they needed little attention until they were served. By that time, all the flavours were deliciously merged. Cooking everything in ten minutes, so necessary now yet always so fraught, was unknown.

Meat dishes should always be accompanied by fresh vegetables and perhaps a light salad.

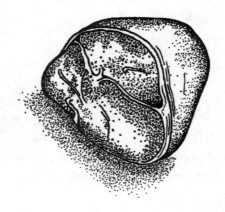

Boiled Corned Beef with Carrots and Dumplings

This wholesome dish is appetising in cold weather and was the traditional St Patrick's Day dinner.

Serves 4.

900 g/2 lb tail-end (brisket) of corned beef
50 g/2 oz/4 US tbsp brown sugar
small onion, sliced
sprig of mint
450 g/1 lb carrots, in large chunks
8 simmered dumplings (optional, page 45)

Cover the beef with water and bring it slowly to the boil. Simmer for 1 hour. Skim the liquid.

Put the brown sugar, onion, mint and carrots into the water and simmer very gently for another hour.

For the last 20 minutes of cooking, place the dumplings on top of the meat and vegetables. Cover and simmer very gently. The dumplings will swell but should be light.

Serve hot with separately-cooked cabbage and potatoes in their skins.

Save the stock for lentil or potato soup (pages 6 and 5).

Chicken Pot Roast

Originally made with an old bird, this will make any chicken moist and well-flavoured, hot or cold.

Serves 4.

1 chicken
flour to sprinkle
butter for browning
3 rashers (slices) of bacon
2 leeks, chopped
6 sticks celery, chopped
2 large carrots, chopped
rosemary
thyme

Sprinkle the bird with flour. Brown the bird all over in the butter and pour away the fat. Place in a deep casserole dish and cover with bacon slices. Push all the chopped vegetables and herbs down around it. Add stock, if necessary, and cover.

Simmer gently for 1 hour or more, turning the bird over from time to time.

Crisp up the breast by removing the lid. Then put the bird on a plate surrounded by the vegetables.

Chicken can also be pot-roasted using just onions and tomatoes. The tomatoes should be skinned and sliced. They will produce a sauce to pass around with the chicken.

Irish Stew

This invaluable stew will cook itself while you are out shopping.
It will be ready on your return.

Serves 4.

potatoes ⎫ amounts according
leeks or onions ⎭ to personal taste
2 large carrots
6 thick loin lamb chops, trimmed and cubed
thyme
parsley

Slice the potatoes and cut the other vegetables into a large dice. Make a layer of vegetables at the bottom of a thick-based saucepan.

Cut any bones out of the meat and throw these into a little boiling water to make a quick stock.

Put a layer of the prepared meat over the vegetables. Continue the layers. The top one should be potatoes.

Pour water and stock to three-quarters up the meat and vegetables. Simmer very gently for 2 hours.

Remove the meat and vegetables with a slotted spoon and put in a warm casserole dish.

Reduce the liquid by half to thicken. Add at least 1 dsp/1½ US tbsp each of thyme and parsley. Pour this sauce over the meat and serve at once.

Lancashire Hotpot

Serves 4.

1.35 kg/3 lb potatoes
1 large onion
4 side loin lamb chops
4 lamb kidneys
225 g/8 oz flat mushrooms } optional
salt and pepper
25 g/1 oz/¼ stick butter or margarine, melted
parsley

Slice the potatoes and onion and put a layer of them at the bottom of a pie dish.

Trim the chops into neat pieces, removing fat or bones. The bones can be put into boiling water to make a quick stock.

Lay some chops over the potatoes and onions, then slices of kidney and mushroom. Repeat these layers, sprinkling occasionally with salt and pepper and finishing with a smooth layer of sliced potatoes.

Add 280 ml/½ pint/1¼ cups of the warm stock. Brush over with melted butter or margarine and cover with buttered tinfoil. Cook in a moderate oven (180°C/350°F/gas 4) for at least 2 hours.

Take the tinfoil off for the last ½ hour to make the potatoes crisp and brown. Add more stock if it is necessary. Sprinkle with parsley and serve at once.

This can be made without kidneys and mushrooms.

Roast Duck with Sage Stuffing

*A free-range duck (if possible), cooked traditionally
with a hearty stuffing.*
Serves 4.

1 duck, 2-2¼ kg/4½-5 lb
3 onions
175 g/6 oz/3 cups soft white breadcrumbs
several fresh sage leaves, chopped
1 egg
salt and pepper
sprinkling of flour

S lice the onions and boil them for 20 minutes. Chop them up and mix with the breadcrumbs and chopped sage leaves. Bind with an egg and season. Put the stuffing into the bird.

If the duck is farmed, it may be too fat. If so, cut a lot of the loose fat off and prick the bird all over. Sprinkle it with flour. Stuff it with the breadcrumb mixture. Tie the legs and wings.

Roast in the oven at 200°C/400°F/gas 6 for 15 minutes per pound (30 minutes per kg) and 15 minutes over, turning the bird every 20 minutes and continuing to prick the skin.

Pour off most of the fat in the roasting pan at least twice during the cooking and sprinkle flour on the remaining drippings.

When finished, the duck skin should be brown and crisp. The juices should run clear (not pink) if you put in a carving fork.

Finish the gravy and serve the duck with plenty of apple sauce and, in season, new potatoes and peas, both cooked with mint.

A potato stuffing can also be used (page 46).

Steak and Kidney Pudding*

A well-flavoured old-style pudding that needs long cooking.
Serves 4.

350 g/12 oz suet crust (page 53)
350 g/12 oz tender stewing steak
2 beef kidneys
a little seasoned flour
herbs
extra stock

M ake a suet crust. Break off a quarter of the dough and set aside. Roll out the remainder and line a 15 cm/6" china pudding bowl/casserole dish. Let the pastry overlap the rim a little.

Cut the meat into bite-sized pieces and sprinkle with seasoned flour and a teaspoon of chopped herbs. Pack the meat loosely into the pastry. Pour water to halfway up the meat and make a lid out of the remaining dough. Wet the edges to seal them. Cover with 2 layers of tinfoil and tie securely with string.

Put the bowl into a saucepan with boiling water coming three-quarters of the way up the sides. Keep the water on the boil for 3 hours, replenishing when needed.

Do not try to turn out this pudding. Serve it from its own bowl straight onto the plates. A little extra hot stock can be poured into the bowl at this stage.

In Ireland, 'pudding' often refers to a savoury meat dish.
The word may also refer to the dessert course.

Toad-in-the-Hole

Excellent for outdoor people. Thyme gives
the batter a special flavour.
Serves 4.

150 g/5 oz/1¼ cups plain (all-purpose) flour
2 large eggs
280 ml/½ pint/1¼ cups liquid (3 parts milk, 1 part water)
1 level dsp/1½ US tbsp thyme
450 g/1 lb sausages*

Put the flour into a mixing bowl. Break the eggs into the middle and mix with a wooden spoon.

Add the liquid gradually, beating all the time, until the mixture is smooth. Sprinkle in the thyme.

Halve and skin the sausages (if necessary). Put them in a baking tin or shallow casserole and heat this well in the oven.

Pour the batter over the sausages and put the dish back in the oven at 200°C/400°F/gas 6. The heat can be reduced a little after 20 minutes, but watch it — batter is unpredictable. The dish should be ready in 40 minutes.

Serve immediately with French mustard or horseradish sauce (page 86).

While brown-and-serve sausages could be used, American readers will get a tastier result with bockwurst or bratwurst, sliced into 2" pieces.

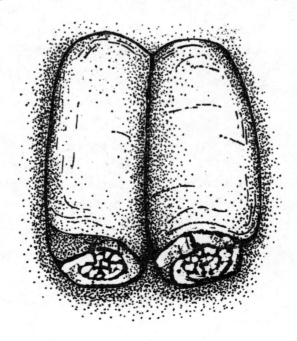

Stuffed Fillets of Pork

*These excellent cuts, an Irish speciality, remain moist if
they are wrapped in bacon rashers/slices.*
Serves 4.

2 pork fillets*
350 g/¾ lb potato stuffing (page 46)
4 back rashers (slices) of bacon, thinly cut

Put the fillets on a board and hammer them with a rolling
pin to make them flatter. Trim off any fat.

Spread the potato stuffing on top of one fillet. Place the
other fillet over the stuffing and wrap the stuffed fillets tightly
together in the bacon rashers/slices. Roast in a moderate oven
(200°C/400°F/gas 6) for about 1½ hours.

Serve hot with gravy and apple sauce (page 84).

Americans will need a loin cut, flattened out to resemble a flank steak.

Roast Beef

*On special occasions, Irish families enjoyed roast beef, usually
from Westmeath or another midland county. A sirloin, well hung
by your favourite butcher, was boned and rolled for you.
It is almost as tasty cold as hot. It is best when pink in the middle.*
Serves 4.

❧

2¼ kg/5 lb sirloin of beef
seasoned flour, to dust over it and for the gravy
1 dsp/1½ US tbsp olive oil (prevents sticking
to the roasting tin)

Take the beef out of the fridge an hour before you start to cook it. This softens it a little.

Pour the olive oil into a roasting tin. Heat this in the oven at 190°C/400°F/gas 6. Flour the beef very lightly and place it in the hot roasting tin. Roast at this temperature for 15 minutes. Then lower the oven to 180°C/350°F/gas 4 for the rest of the roasting time.

Roast for at least 15 minutes to the pound (30 minutes per kg) and 15 over.

After ½ hour, some juice will have run out of the meat into the roasting tin. Shake 1 dsp/1½ US tbsp of flour into this to lay a foundation for the gravy. At the same time, turn the meat over to make the juices spread evenly. (For the gravy at this stage, see page 43.)

Turn the beef every now and then. About ½ hour before the meat is finished, spoon some of the juices into another tin for Yorkshire pudding (page 46).

When the beef has cooked for the allotted time, test it with a carving fork. If the skin is crisp and the juices run just a little pink when you put the fork right inside, the beef is done. It can be dished up surrounded by pieces of Yorkshire pudding.

Serve with horseradish sauce (page 86).

Cottage Pie

A favourite with all. The meat should be moist and well flavoured,
the potato creamy. This melts in the mouth.
Serves 4.

675 g/1½ lb cooked beef or lamb
4 tomatoes, skinned
3 rashers (slices) of lean bacon
thyme, salt and pepper to taste
1 dsp/1½ US tbsp mango chutney
675 g/1½ lb potatoes
50 g/2 oz/½ stick butter
hot milk

Mince/grind the cooked meat, tomatoes and bacon. (Your butcher may oblige you by doing this.)

Add the herbs and chutney. The mixture should be a thick, dropping consistency, although you may need to add some well-flavoured stock.

Put in a shallow casserole and keep warm.

Cook the potatoes and mash them with butter and hot milk until they are creamy, almost liquid. Spread them over the meat mixture. Scatter slivers of butter over the top.

Bake in the oven at 200°C/400°F/gas 6 until it is golden-brown on top and sizzling underneath, about 35 minutes.

Braised Beef in Guinness

Guinness gives body and flavour to this nourishing cut of beef.
Serves 4.

675 g/1½ lb top side of beef
a little olive oil or vegetable oil for browning
10 spring onions ⎫
3 large carrots ⎬ roughly chopped
225 g/½ lb mushrooms ⎭
salt and pepper
1 dsp/1½ US tbsp thyme
280 ml/½ pint/1¼ cups Guinness

Brown the meat quickly in the olive oil. Reduce the heat and remove the meat. Slightly brown the onions, carrots and half the mushrooms.

Put the vegetable mixture in a heavy casserole dish and place the meat on top of the vegetables. Add the seasoning, thyme and Guinness.

Simmer gently until the meat is tender, about 2 hours, stirring occasionally. Twenty minutes before serving, add the remaining mushrooms.

Serve with steamed potatoes and a green vegetable, such as cabbage or runner/green beans.

&

Brown Stew with Guinness

A little Guinness enriches the taste of this heart-warming stew.
Serves 4.

450 g/1 lb round steak, trimmed and cut into bite-sized pieces
1 tbsp/1¼ US tbsp seasoned flour to coat
salt and pepper
olive or vegetable oil for frying
1 onion, chopped
2 carrots, diced
1 tomato, skinned and chopped
thyme, marjoram and parsley
150 ml/¼ pint/⅔ cup Guinness

Put the flour, a pinch of salt and some pepper in a plastic bag. Shake the pieces of meat in the seasoned flour.

Fry the meat gently until golden-brown, then transfer to a large pan. Fry the onion and carrots lightly in the meat juices. Then add the tomato and Guinness. Add the herbs, reserving a bit of parsley.

Pour the Guinness mixture over the meat. You may need to add a little water to cover everything.

Simmer gently for about 2½ hours, until the meat is tender. Taste the juice half-way through the cooking. Add more salt, if necessary, even some redcurrant jelly.

Sprinkle with the remaining parsley and serve with steamed potatoes or pasta shells or wheels. This stew is also delicious with simmered dumplings (page 45). The dumplings should be dropped into the stew about ½ hour before it is ready.

Roast Lamb with Rosemary

We enjoy Wicklow lamb because we live there.
But lamb from any hilly part of Ireland is equally as good.
Like roast beef, roast lamb is a family treat.
Serves 4.

1 x 1¾ kg/4 lb leg of lamb
seasoned flour for dusting over
sprigs of fresh rosemary
1 dsp/1½ US tbsp flour for the gravy

Dust the leg with seasoned flour.
Make 4 or 5 deep incisions in the leg. Push the rosemary sprigs into these to flavour the meat. (Mint will do if you have no rosemary.)

Put the meat into a hot oven (200°C/400°F/gas 6). After 15 minutes, reduce the heat to 180°C/350°F/gas 4. It should take 20 minutes per pound (30 minutes per kg) and 20 over. Lamb is most popular when a light pink in the middle. Turn the lamb several times during roasting.

After ½ hour, put 1 dsp/1½ US tbsp flour in the tin to make a basis for gravy. Continue with instructions for the gravy on page 43.

When the lamb is cooked, put it in a warm oven while you finish making the gravy.

Serve with mint sauce or mint jelly (page 85).

Dublin Coddle

This traditional dish is a favourite with hungry young men,
especially on a rainy Saturday night.
Serves 4.

6 rashers (slices) of lean bacon
450 g/1 lb sausages*, pricked
675 g/1½ lb potatoes
1 onion
1 large apple
1 tbsp/1¼ US tbsp parsley

B ring the rashers and sausages to the boil in water and
simmer for 5 minutes. Pour the stock into a jug.

Peel the potatoes, onion and apple and chop into a dice.

Arrange some of the vegetables, apple and parsley at the
bottom of a saucepan. Then spread on a layer of sausages and
bacon. Continue this in layers until everything is used.

Pour the stock over all and bring slowly to the boil.
Simmer until the vegetables are soft.

Lift the coddle onto a casserole dish using a slotted
spoon. Keep it warm. Reduce the stock by boiling it quickly
and pour some of it over the coddle.

Serve at once.

Americans should try cocktail sausages.

Bacon and Cabbage

*This is the most traditional and wholesome of Irish family meals.
It was especially appreciated in the farming community where
many people would cure their own bacon and grow their
own cabbage. Both would be simmered together for a long time
in a large pot and the two tastes merged. Potatoes in their
skins were always cooked separately.
Nowadays, we like cooking vegetables more quickly, so the
cabbage for this dish is usually boiled just before the meal.
However, if some of the bacon water is used for this, we have
the authentic bacon and cabbage taste.*

Serves 4.

900 g/2 lb lean bacon*
1 head of cabbage, chopped roughly
browned breadcrumbs

B ring the bacon slowly to the boil in enough water to
cover. Skim the water lightly and simmer carefully for
about 1½ hours. When tender, keep the bacon in a warm
place in its water.

Take 115 ml/4 oz/½ cup of the bacon water and the
same amount of tap water and bring to the boil. Throw in the
cabbage and cook it quickly. Drain well.

Sprinkle the bacon with browned breadcrumbs and
serve everything very hot with parsley sauce (page 87).

Americans should use bacon belly, including the rind, or a boiling ham.

Ways with Potatoes

Champ
Colcannon
Bubble-and-Squeak
Potato Cakes

Potatoes are usually cooked in their skins in Ireland. They are either boiled, then steamed off with a cloth over them, or else baked in a moderate oven for 1½ hours. This way of cooking gives potatoes an earthy flavour and pleases nutritionists who claim that all the vitamins are next to the skin. The potatoes are served on separate side plates and everyone peels their own.

There are simple, traditional ways of enlivening potatoes. One of the most delicious is champ, often eaten as a meal in itself.

Champ

Champ is a Northern Irish dish. I learned of it from our old friend
Sophie, who came from there. She also called it 'nests',
saying that children, especially small ones, loved it, and indeed
they do. Though Sophie made champ with potato
sprinkled with carrot, most people use spring onion or chive with
the potato, giving it much more flavour. Champ must be
eaten very hot, with the butter melting in front of your eyes.
Serves 4.

675 g/1½ lb potatoes, peeled
6 spring onions (or a bunch of chives)
hot milk
1 tsp salt
butter for melting

B oil or steam the potatoes. If you dislike raw onion, chop
the spring onions and cook them with the potatoes.

Mash the potatoes and onions. When they are
thoroughly mashed, gradually add enough hot milk to make
the potatoes into a cream. Season with salt.

Keeping the mixture very hot, form it into piles on
individual hot plates. Press a crater shape in the top of the
pile and put a slab of butter into this to melt.

Children and many others like to eat champ by forking
up a mouthful of potato from the edge of the pile and dipping
it into the melted butter. The taste is succulent.

Colcannon

Colcannon is one of the most traditional of Irish foods, usually eaten on Hallowe'en but often at other times too. At Hallowe'en, a ring would be pushed into the potato mixture to make prophecies of marriage which resulted in general excitement.

Serves 4.

900 g/2 lb potatoes, peeled
1 onion, chopped finely or 6 spring onions
2 leaves of kale*, chopped
50 g/2 oz/½ stick butter or margarine
milk, warmed
salt and pepper

Cut up the potatoes and chop the onion finely. Put both into a steamer and cook until soft.

Cook the kale* quickly in another saucepan.

Mash the potato and onion and add the well-chopped kale. Add the butter. Season to taste.

Add the warm milk gradually, keeping it warm in the saucepan as you whip the mixture with a fork. When it is soft, creamy and piping hot, put it straight onto the plates.

Serve it with rashers/slices of bacon or lamb chops.

*Kale is a member of the cabbage family with dark green, curly leaves which do not form a head. Savoy cabbage is a good substitute where kale is unavailable.

Bubble-and-Squeak

This was surely invented as a way of using up left-over cabbage.
It is called bubble-and-squeak because the vegetables are boiled
first or bubbled. They then squeak after they are fried.
If care is taken and the mixture is cooked to a golden-brown
crispness, it is attractive to young appetites.
Serves 2.

450 g/1 lb potatoes, peeled
175 g/6 oz cooked cabbage, chopped
salt and pepper
butter or margarine for frying

This tastes better if the potatoes are freshly cooked. Steam or boil, dry off and then mash the potatoes. Add the chopped cabbage and seasoning. Do not add milk, as it will leak into the frying pan.

Press the potato and cabbage mixture into one or two 'cakes' for each person. Fry these until there is a crisp brown skin on both sides. Serve at once.

Potato Cakes

*These are delicious for a family tea, served very hot
with a knob of butter melting over them.*
Serves 4.

350 g/12 oz/¾ lb potatoes
2 tbsp/2½ US tbsp self-raising flour
25 g/1 oz/¼ stick butter

B oil or steam the potatoes. Mash them without milk and
cool them.

Rub the butter into the flour. Mix this well with the
mashed potato. Season to taste. Knead into a flexible dough,
adding a little more flour if necessary.

Either roll the dough on a pastry board and cut it into
rounds, or form it with your hands into several flat cakes. The
latter is less trouble and less wasteful.

Fry the cakes in a little butter until they are dry and a
nice brown colour.

Extras

Roast Meat Gravy
Forcemeat Balls
Roast Savoury Dumplings
Simmered Dumplings
Potato Stuffing
Yorkshire Pudding
Cheese Fingers
Tomatoes in Vinaigrette Dressing
Herb Butter

Families often like the extras best.

Long cooking enhances the taste of roast meat gravy, and savoury dumplings or forcemeat balls are delicious accompaniments. People still grow their own sage, thyme and parsley to mix into dumplings and stuffings.

It is not hard to grow fresh herbs for your extras and they taste especially pungent when freshly picked. Just a few of the best-known herbs — thyme, sage, marjoram and rosemary — give food a great lift. Conveniently, all seem to like the same growing conditions, plenty of sun and warmth. Parsley is harder to please but is indispensable and is now available in most greengrocers. Mint is easy to grow, but it must be contained to stop it from spreading everywhere. Plant all of these as near the kitchen as you can.

Roast Meat Gravy

Gravy should never be floury or lumpy when made this way.
It also tastes genuinely of the roast meat.

Put your meat in the oven to roast. When the juices have run, in about 20 minutes, sprinkle 1 dsp/1½ US tbsp of seasoned flour over the floor of the roasting pan.

About 20 minutes later, the flour will have browned. Now pour in 2 tbsp/2½ US tbsp of boiling water or stock. This gives a meaty foundation to the gravy.

When the meat is cooked and resting in a warm place, stir hot water or stock (carrot water is ideal) into the pan. Put in a little more than you need and let it reduce.

Forcemeat Balls

Savoury with any roast.

125 g/4 oz/1 cup white breadcrumbs
1 rasher (slice) bacon, finely chopped
2 tbsp/2½ US tbsp green herbs, chopped
25 g/1 oz/¼ stick butter, melted
2 eggs, beaten
flour to bind

Mix the breadcrumbs with the bacon and herbs. Pour in the melted butter and mix. Bind by stirring in the eggs and a little flour. Make the mixture into balls of 4 cm/1½" in diameter. Do this with floury fingers.

Put the forcemeat balls into the roasting tin when the meat juices have run. Turn them over once or twice until they are pale brown.

Roast Savoury Dumplings

Typical dumplings are round, white and cooked in a stew.
These are flat, roasted and crisp.

175 g/6 oz/1½ cups plain (all-purpose) flour
75 g/3 oz/6 US tbsp Atora (grated) suet
1 tbsp/1¼ US tbsp leek, finely chopped
salt
water

Mix the suet with the flour. Add the leek and a little salt, forming into a dough with water.

Form into cakes about 5 cm/2" square and 1¼ cm/2" deep.

Put into the roasting pan when the meat has 1 hour to cook, the tin is hot and the juices have started to run.

Turn the dumplings over once. They should be a rich brown and very crisp.

Simmered Dumplings

These are cooked with boiled beef or beef stew (page 33).
Made with self-raising flour, they should not be heavy.

225 g/8 oz/2 cups self-raising flour
125 g/4 oz/¼ cup grated suet (preferably Atora)
½ tsp salt (if needed — not if cooking salt beef)
1 dsp/1¼ US tbsp thyme and parsley, chopped
cold water

Mix the flour, suet, salt and herbs together. Bind with a little water and shape into 6 small balls with floured fingers.

Place on top of the stew. Cover and cook for 20-25 minutes. The dumplings will rise, be light and take the taste of the meat and vegetables.

Potato Stuffing

A popular stuffing for stuffed fillets of pork (page 30),
for roast duck (page 25), or even for goose.

350 g/12 oz potatoes, peeled
1 large onion, chopped (or several spring onions)
3 or 4 sage leaves, chopped
15 g/½ oz/1 US tbsp butter, melted
salt and pepper

B oil or steam the potatoes, onion and sage leaves together
until the potatoes are cooked.

Mash the potatoes with the onion and sage. Add the
melted butter and mix well. Season to taste.

On no account should you add any milk.

Yorkshire Pudding

This savoury companion to roast beef (page 30) was
adopted gladly by Irish families many years ago. It should be crisp
and piping hot, tasting deliciously of beef dripping.
It is vital to pour the mixture into a very hot baking tin. The basic
ingredients are the same as for toad-in-the-hole.

150 g/5 oz/1¼ cups plain (all-purpose) flour
a pinch of salt
2 large eggs
280 ml/½ pint/1¼ cups liquid (¾ milk and ¼ water)

Measure the flour into a large mixing bowl. Sprinkle with the salt and break the eggs one by one into a well in the centre. Mix well with a wooden spoon. Mix in the liquid gradually, beating all the time. It should be a thick pouring consistency.

About 35 minutes before the beef finishes roasting, take 2 large tablespoons of dripping from the roasting pan and put them in a heated baking tin. When the tin and dripping are very hot, pour in the batter and cook for 30 minutes with the oven at 200°C/400°F/gas 6. Watch it: the pudding will swell, heave and brown.

Cut it into 4 portions and place round the beef.

Some people pour the batter straight into the beef's roasting pan. This makes the pudding taste of the meat juices but uses them up almost entirely, leaving nothing for gravy.

Cheese Fingers

A hearty version of the more elegant cheese straws,
and more quickly made.

225 g/8 oz/2 sticks butter
350 g/12 oz/3 cups self-raising flour
175 /6 oz/1½ cups hard cheese, finely grated
2 tsp/2½ US tsp salt
2 tsp/2½ US tsp dry mustard
a sprinkle of pepper
2 egg yolks

Melt the butter slowly in a large saucepan. *Do not let it boil.* Add the flour and mix well. Add the cheese, salt, dry mustard and pepper. Bind the mixture with the egg yolks. It should become a solid mass.

Press into a Swiss roll/jelly roll tin. Smooth with a knife and prick it well all over with a fork.

Bake at 200°C/400°F/gas 6 for 15 minutes or until it is golden brown and shrinks from the side of the tin.

Mark into 5 cm/2" fingers and take them out of the tin when they are cool. Spread them on a wire rack.

Serve, reheated, with drinks.

&

Tomatoes in Vinaigrette Dressing

To accompany the meat or fish recipes in this book, all substantial,
it is best to serve a simple salad with a light dressing.
The most delicious tomatoes are those taken warm, ripe and sweet
from a cold greenhouse and eaten immediately.
Not many of us are lucky enough to taste these perfect fruits,
but this recipe gives a gallant attempt at the same flavour.
My mother made vinaigrette in just the way I describe, using the
deep wooden spoon from the salad service. I used to love watching
her. If you prefer, mix the dressing in a little bowl.

4 tomatoes
2 tsp/2½ US tsp caster (superfine) sugar
2 tsp salt
2 tsp mustard
2 level tsp/2½ US tsp malt vinegar
2 tbsp/2½ US tbsp extra virgin olive oil
1 tsp fresh herbs

S lice the tomatoes very thinly at least 1 hour before your meal. Arrange them overlapping in a dish. Sift 1½ teaspoons caster/superfine sugar over them and leave at room temperature. The sugar will soak in and become liquid.

Ten minutes before you start eating, put the salt, mustard and remaining sugar into the wooden spoon. Add

49

the vinegar and mix everything together. Fill the spoon slowly with olive oil, mixing all the time. Pour this carefully over the tomatoes. Fill the spoon again with olive oil, along with any fresh herbs you choose, and pour over again.

In a few minutes the tomatoes will be dripping and juicy and have a delicately piquant flavour.

At the bottom of the serving dish there will be a few tablespoonsful of refreshing juice. We mop this up with plain homemade bread.

Some people may find this dressing too bland. They need only increase the amount of salt, mustard and vinegar.

This tomato salad can hold its own as a separate course.

Herb Butter

*Herb butter is simply made. It is mouth-watering when it melts
over hot vegetables, on piping-hot fish or meat, or even when
spread, softened, on homemade bread. Chives and
parsley taste good in herb butter, as do thyme and marjoram.
Rosemary is too tough and sage too strongly flavoured.*

85 g/3 oz/¾ stick butter, softened
a few drops lemon juice
1 tbsp/1½ US tbsp chopped herbs, freshly picked
(preferably a mixture of at least 2 kinds)

B eat the butter and lemon juice with a fork. Add the
finely-chopped herbs and beat again.

If you wish to put it on hot food, form it into a flat
shape and place this in the fridge to harden. Divide this into
slabs as you use it. It will keep for a few days.

Keep the herb butter soft for spreading straight onto
homemade bread. Or you can make popular herb bread by
pushing the butter down incisions in a French roll.

Pastry

ﮔ

Suet Crust
Rich Shortcrust Pastry
Rough Puff Pastry

We can buy pastry ready-made now, both shortcrust and puff pastry. We have all done this, thankfully. As well as being so labour-saving, bought pastry never seems to fall to pieces or collapse, as our own can do.

But anyone who has time and enthusiasm to work at pastry-making finds it rewarding and not too hard. Shortcrust pastry made with fresh butter and egg yolk has a golden look and a melting quality, and homemade rough puff pastry is deliciously flaky.

Making good pastry is both a skill and an achievement.

Suet Crust

175 g/6 oz/1½ cups plain (all-purpose) flour
75 g/3 oz/6 US tbsp Atora (grated) suet
water
salt to taste

Add the suet to the flour and mix lightly with a wooden spoon. Add salt and just enough water to make a flexible dough.

Roll out on a floured board.

Some cooks use self-raising flour. This makes a light but thick crust which is rather soft.

About 25 g/1 oz/1 US tbsp caster/superfine sugar can be added to the flour-suet mixture if the recipe is sweet.

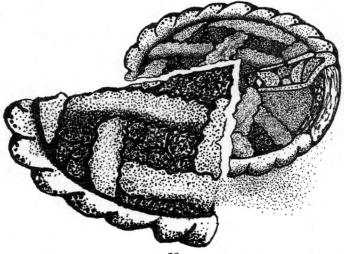

Rich Shortcrust Pastry

A pastry that will do well for any pie or tart.

225 g/8 oz/2 cups plain (all-purpose) flour
150 g/5 oz/1¼ sticks butter and margarine, mixed
1 or 2 egg yolks
a little water
1 dsp/1½ US tbsp caster (superfine) sugar
(if the filling is sweet)

Rub the butter and margarine into the flour until it resembles breadcrumbs.

Add the caster sugar if you are using it.

Work in the egg yolk(s) and water until the pastry leaves the sides of the bowl cleanly.

Knead slightly until it is pliable.

Roll it carefully on a floured board, giving it several half turns.

Rough Puff Pastry

This flaky pastry is easier to make than many people think.
It tastes and looks very professional. Take the butter out of the
fridge at least ½ hour before you start mixing it in.

225 g/8 oz/2 cups plain (all-purpose) flour
pinch of salt
¼ tsp lemon juice
150 g/5 oz/1¼ sticks butter, cut into walnut-sized pieces
water

Put the flour and salt into a mixing bowl and flick your fingers through to air it. Add the lemon juice.

Add the pieces of butter. Mix quickly and add just enough cold water to bind it together. Do all this with a flexible knife or palette knife.

Turn the dough onto a well-floured board and roll it into an oblong piece. Sprinkle a little flour on this and fold it into thirds. Give the pastry a half turn, seeing that the board is still well floured to avoid sticking.

Repeat this rolling and turning two or three times and then make your pie.

Hot Puddings

Apple Amber
Apple Dumpling
Bread-and-Butter Pudding
Rice Pudding
Steamed Sponge
Treacle Tart
Roly-Poly Pudding
Spicy Baked Apples
Pancakes

As all of us in Ireland used to live in cold houses, warm and cosy puddings, sometimes sweetened with sugared fruit, were important to us.

When houses became warmer, puddings went out of fashion. They have made a comeback lately, not for every day but for occasions and at weekends. Cooks often express their individuality with ordinary wholesome puddings, cooked with care.

Puddings made with fresh ingredients are not unhealthy — far from it. And they can always be followed by the fresh fruit so necessary to us.

Apple Amber

Serves 4.

4 large cooking apples, peeled and sliced
25 g/1 oz/¼ stick butter or margarine
juice of 1 orange
125 g/4 oz/½ cup brown sugar
1 tsp/1¼ US tsp coriander
1 tsp/1¼ US tsp cinnamon
4 eggs, separated
125 g/4 oz/½ cup granulated sugar

Cook the apples in the butter or margarine and the orange juice until they will mash easily. Add the brown sugar, coriander and cinnamon.

When all is cooked and well mixed, remove from the heat and mix in the beaten egg yolks. The apples should now be a golden colour. Place the apple mixture in an oven-proof dish and keep warm.

Whip up the egg whites until they are stiff. Fold in the granulated sugar with a metal spoon. Dollop the whites on top of the apple mixture in rough hillocks.

Put into a warm oven (180°C/350°F/gas 4) until the egg white is brown. Then leave in a cool oven (140°C/275°F/gas 1) for an hour or longer.

Apple Dumpling

*Economical and satisfying, an excellent follow-on
for a light first course.*

Serves 4.

350 g/¾ lb sweetened suet crust (page 53)
cooking apples, preferably Bramley
125 g/4 oz/1 cup brown sugar
cinnamon
juice of ½ orange

Divide the suet dough into two-thirds and one-third.
Roll out the larger piece and line a 15 cm/6" pudding
bowl/round-sided plastic bowl. Fill the hollow well with sliced
apples, sprinkled liberally with brown sugar, and add a
teaspoon of cinnamon.

Pour the juice of half an orange or 2 tbsp of water over
the fruit.

Make the remaining dough into a lid, wetting the edges
to join the bowl lining. Cover this with two layers of tinfoil
and tie securely.

Put the bowl in a saucepan with boiling water coming
three-quarters of the way up the bowl. Cook for 2½-3 hours,
replenishing the water if necessary.

After uncovering the tinfoil, put a knife around the
pudding and turn it out onto a hot plate. Serve with brown
sugar and cream.

Plums or blackberries can be cooked with the apple,
making a stronger flavour.

Bread-and-Butter Pudding

*The secret of a well-made bread-and-butter pudding
is to use bread sparingly.*
Serves 4.

4 slices of white bread, crusts removed and buttered
3 dsp/4½ US tbsp caster (superfine) sugar
125 g/4 oz/1 cup sultanas* or fruit mix
(to include candied peel)
3 eggs
1 tsp/1¼ US tsp cinnamon
600 ml/1 pint/2½ cups milk

Spread the crustless bread with soft butter. Put two slices at the bottom of a casserole dish. Sprinkle with half the caster/superfine sugar and half the dried fruit.

Repeat this once.

Beat the eggs with the remaining caster/superfine sugar. Add the cinnamon.

Heat the milk and add it to the egg mixture, stirring first, then beating. When it is well beaten, pour it over the bread, covering it. Leave this for at least ½ hour.

Stand your casserole in a baking tin holding about 5 cm/2" of hot water.

Cook in the oven at 180°C/350°F/gas 4 until the top is golden-brown and the custard set, about ¾ hour.

Serve with pouring cream.

*Yellow raisins (dried green grapes)

Rice Pudding

Rice pudding has an atrocious reputation because it is often
carelessly cooked. Correctly done, it should be sweet and creamy.
Serves 4.

75 g/3 oz/½ cup round-grain rice*
1.2 L/2 pints/5 cups full cream milk
75 g/3 oz/3 US tbsp demerara (granulated brown) sugar
a little cinnamon or coriander
15 g/½ oz/½ stick butter

Soak the rice in the milk for 2 hours in the dish you will use to cook it.

Stir in the sugar and cinnamon/coriander. Put slivers of butter over the top.

Bake slowly in a very low oven for 2½-3 hours. For the first hour, stir the pudding occasionally.

If the oven is too hot, put the pudding into a baking tin of warm water.

Serve with cream and brown sugar.

*Italian short-grain (Arborio) is recommended.

Steamed Sponge

*This is usually made with golden/Karo syrup in the bottom
of the bowl and served with a syrup sauce.
It can also be spread over stewed apple and put in the oven,
making Eve's Pudding.
Serves 4.*

4 dsp/6 US tbsp golden (Karo) syrup
125 g/4 oz/1 stick butter or margarine
75 g/3 oz/3 US tbsp caster (superfine) sugar
2 eggs, beaten
175 g/6 oz/1½ cups plain (all-purpose) flour ⎫
1½ tsp/1¾ US tsp baking powder ⎭ mixed
a little milk

Put the golden/Karo syrup in the bottom of the bowl in
which you are cooking the sponge.

Cream the butter and sugar until very soft. Beat in the
eggs one at a time. Sprinkle in a little flour and mix.

Fold in the flour and baking powder mixture gradually
with a metal spoon. Add a tablespoon or two of milk.

Fill a pudding bowl/round-sided plastic bowl two-thirds
full with the mixture. Cover with tinfoil and tie it securely.

Put the bowl in a saucepan with boiling water coming
⅔ up the side. Cook for 2 hours, topping up the water when
needed. The pudding should be light to taste and an
attractive yellow colour.

Serve with a warm sauce made with 1 dsp/1½ US tbsp
golden/Karo syrup dissolved in a little warm water.

ء

Treacle Tart

Popular with all ages.
Serves 4.

225 g/8 oz rich shortcrust pastry (page 54)
150 g/5 oz/2½ cups white breadcrumbs
juice of ½ lemon
a little lemon rind
golden (Karo) syrup (enough to make a thick dropping
consistency when mixed with the breadcrumbs)
beaten egg

M ix the breadcrumbs with the lemon juice and rind and the golden/Karo syrup.

Put the rolled-out pastry into a tart pan/pie dish, saving about ⅓ of it. Fill with the breadcrumb mixture.

Form the left-over pastry into twisted sticks and arrange them over the tart in a lattice pattern. Brush the pastry with egg.

Put the tart into a hot oven (200°C/400°F/gas 6) for 10 minutes. Then reduce to 180°C/350°F/gas 4. If there are any signs of burning, cover it with tinfoil. It will be ready in 30 to 40 minutes.

Treacle tart can also be made with black treacle or with molasses.

Roly-Poly Pudding

For years, my husband begged me to make this pudding but I never did. I thought it had to be boiled in a floured cloth and was afraid that the water would flood into the pudding. Then I started baking roly-poly in the oven very successfully. It is an economical pudding, except for the jam — you need most of a one-pound pot. Serves 4.

225 g/8 oz/2 cups plain (all-purpose) flour
75 g/3 oz/6 US tbsp grated or Atora suet
25 g/1 oz/¼ stick butter, cut in very small pieces
water
350 g/¾ lb jam, gooseberry if possible
milk or beaten egg to brush over

Mix the flour, grated suet and morsels of butter in a bowl. You may have to rub in some of the butter pieces. Bind with a little cold water to make a dough.

Roll the dough out carefully on a floured board to make an oblong rectangle, ⅔ cm/¼" thick.

Spread this thickly with jam up to 1¼ cm/½" from the edge. Roll up the dough like a Swiss/jelly roll. Seal the edges with water.

Wrap the roly-poly loosely in tinfoil to allow for expansion. Bake in the oven at 200°C/400°F/gas 6 for at least ½ hour.

Uncover it, brush with milk or beaten egg and bake for a further 15 minutes at 190°C/375°F/gas 5.

Dissolve some more of the jam in 2 tbsp/2½ US tbsp boiling water for a sauce. Serve hot and hand around the jam sauce.

Spicy Baked Apples

These can be sour and dreary, but are delicious
made in the following way.
Serves 4.

4 large cooking apples
125 g/4 oz/½ cup demerara (granulated brown) sugar
125 g/4 oz/½ cup mixed fruit (including candied peel)
cinnamon
juice of 1 orange
slivers of butter or margarine
a little water

Core the apples generously, making sure there are no cores left. Make a slit round their equators. Put them in a shallow casserole dish with 2 tbsp/2½ US tbsp of water.

Stuff the apples with sugar and dried fruit. Dust with cinnamon. Squeeze orange juice over them. Put a sliver of butter or margarine on each apple.

Bake at 190°C/375°F/gas 5 until soft right through — about 35 minutes. Baste occasionally.

Serve with pouring cream.

Pancakes

*In Ireland, pancakes are not so much a breakfast treat but a
wintertime dessert, especially on Shrove Tuesday or
'Pancake Day', the day before Ash Wednesday, when they are
served after Colcannon (page 39).*
Everyone loves pancakes, but they are exhausting to cook.
*If possible, have two skilled pancake chefs on hand
to keep things moving.*
Serves 3–5.

125 g/4 oz/1 cup plain (all-purpose) flour
pinch of salt
1 egg + 1 egg yolk, beaten
280 ml/½ pint/1¼ cups milk
1 tbsp olive oil
to serve: fresh lemon wedges and caster (superfine) sugar

U se a large mixing bowl. Put in the flour and salt. Mix.
Then make a well in the centre. Pour the beaten egg
and egg yolk into the well. Mix thoroughly.

Slowly add half the milk, beating all the time. Add the
oil, continuing to beat. Then beat in the rest of the milk, a
little at a time.

This mixture can be left to improve for ½ hour,
even longer.

When ready to make the pancakes, heat a lightly-oiled
heavy-bottomed frying pan. Sprinkle in a little more olive oil.

When the pan is moderately hot, pour in a generous tablespoonful of the batter. (The pancakes should be quite thin.) Maintaining the moderate heat, shake the pan a bit and turn up the edges to see if the underside is browning. When it is, turn the pancake over. It will be ready in 2 or 3 minutes, all golden brown.

Roll up each pancake and serve immediately. The eager diners will unroll their pancakes, sprinkle them with sugar and lemon juice, roll them back up — and eat!

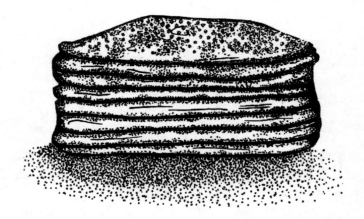

Cold Puddings

Gooseberry Fool
Summer Pudding
Sillabub
Blackberry Ice Cream

It was not often that cold puddings were needed in the old Ireland — usually only in the summer months when the houses became warm at last. Even then, people were happy to substitute fresh strawberries and raspberries, with lots of cream, for any pudding.

No July passed, though, without the aptly named 'Summer Pudding', full of freshly-picked raspberries and redcurrants. The juice soaked through bread all night under a weight, and when it was turned out of its bowl, the pudding was a deep crimson mound. All of summer seemed to be there.

Since gooseberries are the earliest of the soft fruit, gooseberry fool was the first pudding of summer. Sillabub, very rich, was just for special occasions. Ice cream needed buckets and general paraphernalia and was not often made. The simple old recipe for blackberry ice cream is originally from South Carolina.

Gooseberry Fool

Serves 3–5.

180 ml/6 oz/⅔ cup water
125 g/4 oz/½ cup sugar
675 g/1½ lb green gooseberries
2 tbsp/2½ US tbsp ginger wine (optional)
450 ml/¾ pint/2 cups cream

B oil the sugar and water until the sugar is dissolved. Add the topped and tailed gooseberries and cook until soft.

Put through a sieve. Test for sweetness. Add the ginger wine and more sugar, if needed. Let it get quite cold.

Whip the cream and mix it with the gooseberry pulp just before serving.

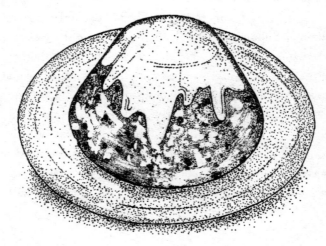

Summer Pudding

redcurrants ⎫
raspberries ⎬ giving amounts
granulated sugar ⎬ is almost impossible!
day-old white bread ⎭

Heat the fruit slowly over low heat. The juice will run, so you will probably need no extra liquid. Cook gently until the fruit is soft and broken down. Add the sugar and stir until it is dissolved. Keep warm.

Cut crusts off the bread. Make it into long, inch-wide pieces and line a pudding bowl/round-sided plastic bowl with these. Pour in some of the fruit mixture.

Make a layer of bread pieces halfway up the bowl. Then pour in the rest of the fruit mixture, reserving some juice. Cover with a layer of bread pieces, which should fill the bowl.

Cover with a plate and put a weight on top of this. The juice may ooze, so put a plate underneath.

Refrigerate for the night. Turn out the next morning and add the remaining juice. The bread should be saturated.

Serve with whipped or pouring cream.

This pudding can be made with blackcurrants, if you like a stronger taste.

Sillabub

This strange name is thought to be old English for
'merry belly'. The recipe is traditional.
Serves 4.

280 ml/½ pint/1¼ cups white wine
juice of 1 lemon and some rind
50 g/2 oz/2 US tbsp caster (superfine) sugar
280 ml/½ pint/1¼ cups cream

Mix the white wine, lemon juice and rind and leave for the night.

Strain into a mixing bowl, add the sugar and stir until it is dissolved.

Whip the cream and add it to the wine mixture. Whip the whole mixture until it is thick and stands up.

Put it into a glass bowl or individual glasses and chill.

Sillabub is sometimes left for 24 hours, allowing the cream to form a curd. It can also be made with sherry or madeira instead of white wine.

Blackberry Ice Cream

Serves 4.

1 pint blackberries
1.2 L/2 pints/5 cups cream
600 ml/1 pint/2½ cups milk
caster (superfine) sugar to taste
juice of a small lemon

Mash the berries and heat them, but do not boil. Squeeze through a cheese cloth or sieve.

Whip the cream and add the milk. Mix into the berries. Add sugar to taste and mix again. Refrigerate.

When ice cold, stir in the lemon juice. Freeze.

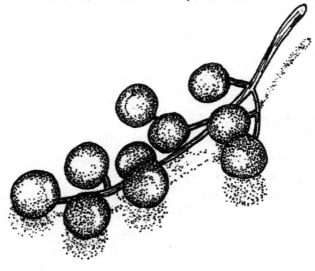

🐦

Preserves and Jams

🐦

Lemon Curd
Strawberry Jam
Almack's Preserve
Marrow, Ginger and Whiskey Jam
Mint Jelly
Gooseberry Jelly with Elderflowers
Light Blackcurrant Jam
Thin Marmalade
Green Tomato Chutney

Many Irishwomen prided themselves on their large cupboards packed with jam, marmalade and jelly, a year's supply.

Those who had a little land grew soft fruit — strawberries, redcurrants, blackcurrants, gooseberries. So large and small houses were pervaded every July with the sharp, sweet smell of summer cooking. In autumn, it was the turn of plums, apples and blackberries. In January, those who had strength after Christmas bought Seville oranges and made the year's marmalade.

The following recipes are versions of familiar preserves, handed down from grandmother to mother to daughter. In spite of the rush of modern life, jam is still made, if not so often.

These jams and marmalade recipes are light and pleasing and economical with fruit. The jellies are subtle and refreshing, the chutney solid but astringent. The lemon curd is ambrosial.

To test for setting

Testing jam or jelly for setting is quite easy. Put a spoonful of the hot jam on a cold plate. Keep this in a cold place for a minute. Then push the sample of jam with your fingernail. If the jam wrinkles, it is set. It can then be poured carefully into warmed jars, as hot jam will crack cold jars.

Jam is usually put into 1-pound pots. To determine the yield of any jam, simply add the weight of the fruit and the weight of the sugar. The yield will be slightly less than the combined weight.

Lemon Curd

A 92-year-old friend, Doris, told me how to make this richly
satisfying spread. It is delicious in tartlets or
on squares of white toast.

125 g/4 oz/1 stick butter or margarine
255 g/9 oz/generous 1 cup granulated sugar
2½ lemons, juice and some grated rind
2 whole eggs, beaten
2 egg yolks

Beat the butter and sugar in a bowl until the mixture is light and soft. Add the lemon juice and rind, beating again.

Put the bowl into a saucepan of boiling water and stir.

Add the beaten eggs and egg yolks gradually, keeping the water on the boil. Stir until thick.

Put into warmed jars. This makes 1½ pounds.

Strawberry Jam

*Strawberry jam was and still is a treat. This is partly because it is
so delicious, made from such a special fruit, and also because we
don't have it often. Strawberries are expensive to buy and harder
to grow than other soft fruit. And they are too sweet to set
properly; we have to add lemon juice. My mother always used
redcurrant juice to set her strawberry jam, 280 ml/½ pint/
1¼ cups to 1.35 kg/3 lb of strawberries. Her jam set well. For
those who don't have redcurrant bushes, the following is
a sound recipe. The strawberries should be dry and
some even a little unripe.*

1¾ kg/4 lb strawberries
juice of 4 lemons
1½ kg/3½ lb sugar, warmed

B ring the strawberries and lemon juice to the boil and
simmer for 20 minutes.

Add the warm sugar. When it is dissolved, start to boil
the jam rapidly. Test for setting (page 73) after 15 minutes.

Yields about 7 one-pound pots.

Almack's Preserve

A very old recipe from an Irish country house.

Take all possible autumn fruit — pears, apples, quinces, plums, blackberries, mulberries. The more variety, the better.

Do not peel the fruit, just wipe thoroughly with a cloth. It is the flesh just under the skin that gives this preserve its unequalled flavour.

Put it in a cool oven for the night to soften into a pulp. Press this through a sieve.

To each 450 g/1 lb/2¼ cups of fruit pulp, add 350 g/ ¾ lb/3 cups sugar. Boil for an hour, stirring to prevent sticking.

Pot it in shallow vessels. It will become solid and can be cut in slices. Serve it cold with cream or ice cream. It tastes like guava jelly.

Marrow, Ginger and Whiskey Jam

Since we have been overrun with courgettes/zucchini, it is hard to find real marrows. You may need to grow them, which is not hard.

1.35 kg/3 lb marrow (zucchini)
1.35 kg/3 lb/6¾ cups sugar
1 cup water
rind and juice of 2 lemons
40 g/1½ oz lump (candied) ginger
cayenne pepper pods
4 oz/½ cup whiskey

Cut the marrow into 5 cm/2" cubes and divide between 2 flat dishes. Cover the cubes with sugar and water and leave overnight for the juices to run. Don't let the dishes overflow!

Put the marrow mixture in the preserving pan with the lemon rind and juice, the ginger and a few cayenne pepper pods tied in muslin. Boil for at least 1 hour. Test for setting (page 73).

When cooked and just off the fire, add whiskey and stir.

Pot into warm jars and cover. A skin does not always form on this jam.

Yields about 6 one-pound pots.

ℳ

Mint Jelly

This should be made with fresh mint.

1.35 kg/3 lb green cooking apples
600 ml/1 pint/2½ cups water
mint stalks
sugar (as below)
juice of 1 lemon
280 ml/½ pint/1¼ cups wine or cider vinegar
½ pint/1¼ cups dry measure of chopped mint leaves
knob of butter

Wash the apples and quarter them. Put in a large pan and add the mint stalks. Simmer slowly to a pulp in the water.

Let the mixture drip through a jelly bag or pillowcase for several hours.

Measure the juice. Bring to the boil. Put in 450 g/ 1 lb/2¼ cups of sugar per 600 ml/1 pint/2½ cups of liquid. Add the lemon juice, vinegar and roughly-chopped mint leaves. Stir over heat until the sugar melts.

Bring to the boil again and boil vigorously until set. Test for setting (page 73) after 5 minutes. When taking off the stove, stir occasionally to stop the mint from sinking. (Put in a knob of butter to help get rid of the scum.)

The delicate tang of this jelly sets off roast lamb and grilled lamb chops.

૨

Gooseberry Jelly with Elderflowers

Elderflowers blossom just as the gooseberries are ripe and the two flavours mingle well.

1¾ kg/4 lb green, slightly unripe gooseberries
1.2 L/2 pints/5 cups water
sugar (as below)
2 or 3 elderflower heads, stems cut off and wrapped in muslin

Simmer the gooseberries gently in the water for 3½-4 hours. Strain through a jelly bag or pillowcase for the night.

Measure the juice. Use 575 g/1¼ lb/2¼ cups of sugar per 600 ml/1 pint/2½ cups of juice.

Bring the juice to the boil again. Drop in the elderflowers in thin muslin wrapping and leave for about 4 minutes, or longer if you like the taste.

Boil the jelly vigorously. Test for setting every few minutes (page 73). If the jelly is set, a skin will form.

Skim, pot and cover.

Light Blackcurrant Jam

This jam is more agreeable than the strong and stodgy blackcurrant jam we find everywhere.

675 g/1½ lb blackcurrants
600 ml/1 pint/2½ cups water
1.35 kg/3 lb/6¾ cups sugar

Grease the preserving pan with margarine or butter. Boil the fruit and water for about 20 minutes, mashing the fruit so it is not hard. Add the sugar, stirring to dissolve it well.

Boil hard after the sugar has dissolved, testing for set after 5 minutes (page 73).

When you have taken the fruit off the stove, stir occasionally before potting to prevent the blackcurrants from sinking.

Yields about 5 one-pound pots.

Thin Marmalade

6 bitter oranges

4 sweet oranges

2 lemons

sugar: 450 g/1 lb per 450 g/1 lb fruit

5 L/9 pints/5 quarts water

Slice the fruit very thinly. Put the pips/pits and thick bits of pith in a separate bowl and cover with water. Soak the fruit in water overnight.

Pour the water from the pip bowl into the preserving pan with the fruit. Simmer the fruit until it is soft.

Add the warmed sugar and boil vigorously until set, about ¾ hour. Test for set (page 73).

Let it stand for 10 minutes before potting and stir several times so that the fruit is well mixed.

Green Tomato Chutney

*Not all the tomato crop ripens in Ireland. There are always
some green ones left on the vines which are usefully made into
chutney, a good foil for cold bacon or corned beef.*

900 g/2 lb green tomatoes
900 g/2 lb green apples
450 g/1 lb shallots
50 g/2 oz/¼ cup garlic
450 g/1 lb/2¼ cups demerara (granulated brown) sugar
225 g/8 oz/1¼ cups sultanas (yellow raisins)
6 red chillies
600 ml/1 pint/2½ cups cider vinegar
15 g/½ oz whole ginger

Quarter the tomatoes. Peel, core and cut the apples in
pieces. Peel the shallots and the garlic. Mix these
ingredients together and put them all through a
mincer/grinder.

Put the mixture into a preserving pan. Add the sugar,
sultanas/raisins, chillies, vinegar and ginger (tied in a small
bag of muslin).

Bring this all slowly to the boil and simmer it gently
until it is thick and soft, about 1¼ hours. Remove the ginger.

Pour the chutney into warm, dry jars and seal it down
as for jam.

Sauces

Apple Sauce
Mint Sauce
Horseradish Sauce
Parsley Sauce
Thick White Sauce

In the old days, sauces were not made very often in Ireland. Stews and boiled salt meats were well flavoured by the vegetables cooked with them. Sauces were looked upon as foreign, and, worse than that, making difficult work just at dishing-up time.

There are, though, some traditional sauces that are still with us, sauces like mint, horseradish and apple. Their astringency contrasts well with the roast meat they accompany. And parsley sauce, so good with boiled bacon or corned beef, is popular with everyone. We cannot make enough of it to satisfy people; they always want more.

The thick white sauce is useful for coating fish or vegetables and for many made-up dishes.

Apple Sauce

The perfect sauce, sweet yet astringent, for roast duck (page 25),
for stuffed fillets of pork (page 30) or for sausages.

2 large apples
juice of ½ orange
1 tsp/1¼ US tsp caster (superfine) sugar

Peel, core and chop up the apples. Put them into a saucepan with the orange juice and sugar. Cook very gently until they are soft, about 10 minutes.

Mash the apples and beat them with a fork. They should become a purée.

Serve the sauce, hot or cold, in a small bowl.

Mint Sauce

This sauce tastes better if the mint is freshly picked.
Serve it with spring lamb.

3 tbsp/3¾ US tbsp chopped fresh mint
1 tbsp/1¼ US tbsp white sugar
boiling water
3 tbsp/3¾ US tbsp vinegar

M ix the mint and sugar in a small but pretty jug, suitable for serving the sauce. Pour in just enough boiling water to cover it. Leave it to settle.

Add your favourite vinegar. Stir it round from time to time.

People will need a small spoon to help themselves to this sauce.

Horseradish Sauce

*A good foil for roast beef and smoked trout. The sauce is made
out of a grated horseradish root, not at all easy to find in
greengrocers' shops and unpopular with gardeners as it spreads so.
If you can find fresh horseradish, do as follows.*

3 tbsp/3¾ US tbsp horseradish roots, peeled and grated
1 dsp/1½ US tbsp vinegar
1 tsp/1¼ US tsp sugar
115 ml/4 oz/½ cup heavy whipping cream

Mix the grated horseradish, vinegar and sugar.
Whip the cream slightly until it just starts to thicken.
Fold the horseradish mixture into the thickened cream.
Turn it all into a ramekin and use within the next ½ hour.

Otherwise, buy a jar of pickled horseradish and mix it
with cream.

ಽ

Parsley Sauce

This simple but popular sauce is relished with boiled bacon or
boiled salt beef. Some people like it with fish. The good taste
of the sauce depends on using parsley lavishly. For family meals,
there's no need to chop finely. Just snip the parsley
with scissors; it's much quicker.

3 tbsp/3¾ US tbsp parsley, chopped roughly
25 g/1 oz/¼ stick butter or margarine
25 g/1 oz/2 US tbsp plain (all-purpose) flour
450 ml/¾ pint/2 cups milk
½ tsp salt

Keeping the chopped parsley beside you, melt the butter gently in a saucepan. Add the flour and mix to a smooth paste.

Add the milk very gradually, stirring carefully all the time. Add the salt.

As soon as the sauce starts to simmer, add ¾ of the parsley and cook for several minutes. The mixture should become thick but pouring.

Add the rest of the parsley, stir, and pour into a very hot sauceboat. Serve at once.

Thick White Sauce

This is made for fish or vegetable pies or for soufflés.

25 g/1 oz/¼ stick butter or margarine
25 g/1 oz/2 US tbsp flour
½ tsp salt
280 ml/½ pint/1¼ cups milk

Melt the butter gently in a small saucepan. Add the flour and salt and stir until blended.

Add the milk very slowly, stirring all the time. After adding half the milk, allow the mixture to boil for a few minutes. Continue adding the milk, letting the sauce simmer from time to time.

When all the milk is blended, simmer the sauce gently for 10 minutes, stirring all the time. It should thicken but should not taste floury.

Index

❧

Almack's Preserve, 76

Amber, Apple, 57

Apple Amber, 57

Apple Dumpling, 58

Apple Sauce, 84

apples

    Apple Amber, 57

    Apple Dumpling, 58

    Apple Sauce, 84

    Mint Jelly, 78

    Spicy Baked Apples, 64

bacon

    Bacon and Cabbage, 36

    Dublin Coddle, 35

    Forcemeat Balls, 43–4

Bacon and Cabbage, 36

Baked Apples, Spicy, 64

Baked Salmon, 18

batter dishes

    Pancakes, 65–6

    Toad-in-the-Hole, 27–8

    Yorkshire Pudding, 46–7

beef

    Boiled Corned Beef

        with Carrots and

        Dumplings, 21

    Braised Beef in Guinness, 32

    Brown Stew

        with Guinness, 33

    Cottage Pie, 31

    Roast Beef, 29–30

    Steak and Kidney

        Pudding, 26–7

Blackberry Ice Cream, 71

Blackcurrant Jam, Light, 80

Boiled Corned Beef with

    Carrots and Dumplings, 21

Braised Beef in Guinness, 32

Bread-and-Butter Pudding, 59

bread dishes

    Bread-and-Butter

        Pudding, 59

    Summer Pudding, 69

breakfasts, Irish, 1–3

Brown Stew with Guinness, 33

Bubble-and-Squeak, 40
Butter, Herb, 51

Cabbage, Bacon and, 36
Champ, 38
Cheese Fingers, 48
chicken
    Chicken Broth, 7
    Chicken Pot Roast, 22
Chicken Pot Roast, 22
chutney
    Green Tomato Chutney, 82
Coddle, Dublin, 19
Colcannon, 39
Cottage Pie, 31
Curd, Lemon, 74

Deep Sea Soup, 8
Dublin Coddle, 35
duck
    Roast Duck with
      Sage Stuffing, 25-6
dumplings
    Apple Dumpling, 58
    Roast Savoury
      Dumplings, 44
    Simmered Dumplings, 45

Family Fish Pie, 14
Fish Cakes, 13
fish dishes, 12-18
    Baked Salmon, 18
    Deep Sea Soup, 8
    Family Fish Pie, 14-15
    Fish Cakes, 13
    Fried Herrings in
      Oatmeal, 16
    Grilled Mackerel, 17
    Special Fish Pie, 15
Fool, Gooseberry, 68
Forcemeat Balls, 43-4
Fried Herrings in Oatmeal, 16
fruit. *see also* apples; jams
    Blackberry Ice Cream, 71
    Gooseberry Fool, 68
    Summer Pudding, 69

Gamekeeper Soup, 10
Gooseberry Fool, 68
Gooseberry Jelly
    with Elderflowers, 79
gravy
    Roast Meat Gravy, 43
Green Tomato Chutney, 82
Grilled Mackerel, 17

Guinness
   Braised Beef in Guinness, 32
   Brown Stew
      with Guinness, 33

Herb Butter, 51
Horseradish Sauce, 86
Hotpot, Lancashire, 24

Ice Cream, Blackberry, 71
Irish Stew, 23

jams, 72–82
   Light Blackcurrant, 80
   Marrow, Ginger
      and Whiskey, 77
   Strawberry, 75
jelly
   Gooseberry,
      with Elderflowers, 79
   Mint, 78

lamb
   Irish Stew, 23
   Lancashire Hotpot, 24
   Roast Lamb with
      Rosemary, 34
   Scotch Broth, 11

Lancashire Hotpot, 24
Lemon Curd, 74
Lentil Soup, 6
Light Blackcurrant Jam, 80

Mackerel, Grilled, 17
Marmalade, Thin, 81
Marrow, Ginger and Whiskey
   Jam, 77
meat dishes, 19–36
   beef, 26–7, 29–33
   corned beef, 21
   Cottage Pie, 31
   lamb, 23, 24, 34
   pork and bacon, 27–9,
      35–6
Mint Jelly, 78
Mint Sauce, 85
Mulligatawny Soup, 9

Pancakes, 65–6
Parsley Sauce, 87
pastry, 52–5
   Rich Shortcrust Pastry, 54
   Rough Puff Pastry, 55
   Suet Crust, 53
pheasant
   Gamekeeper Soup, 10

pies
    Cottage Pie, 31
    Family Fish Pie, 14
    Special Fish Pie, 15
pork
    Stuffed Fillets of Pork, 29
Porridge, 2
Potato Cakes, 41
potatoes, 37–41
    Bubble-and-Squeak, 40
    Champ, 38
    Colcannon, 39
    Cottage Pie, 31
    Fish Cakes, 13
    Potato Cakes, 41
    Potato Soup, 5
    Potato Stuffing, 46
preserves, 72–82
pudding
    Bread-and-Butter
      Pudding, 57
    Rice Pudding, 60
    Roly-Poly Pudding, 63
    Steak and Kidney
      Pudding, 26–7
    Summer Pudding, 57
    Yorkshire Pudding, 46–7

puddings
    cold, 67–71
    hot, 56–66

Rice Pudding, 60
Rich Shortcrust Pastry, 54
Roast Beef, 29–30
Roast Duck with Sage
    Stuffing, 25–6
Roast Lamb with Rosemary, 34
Roast Meat Gravy, 43
Roast Savoury Dumplings, 44
Roly-Poly Pudding, 63
Rough Puff Pastry, 55

Salmon, Baked, 18
sauces, 83–8
    Apple Sauce, 84
    Horseradish Sauce, 86
    Mint Sauce, 85
    Parsley Sauce, 87
    Thick White Sauce, 88
sausages
    Dublin Coddle, 35
    Toad-in-the-Hole, 27–8
Scotch Broth, 11
Shortcrust Pastry, Rich, 54

Sillabub, 70

Simmered Dumplings, 45

soups, 4–11

    Chicken Broth, 7

    Deep Sea Soup, 8

    Gamekeeper Soup, 10

    Lentil Soup, 6

    Mulligatawny Soup, 9

    Potato Soup, 5

    Scotch Broth, 11

Special Fish Pie, 15

Spicy Baked Apples, 64

Sponge, Steamed, 61

sponges

    Steamed Sponge, 61

Steak and Kidney Pudding, 26–7

Steamed Sponge, 61

Stew, Irish, 23

Strawberry Jam, 75

Stuffed Fillets of Pork, 29

stuffing

    Potato Stuffing, 46

Suet Crust, 53

Summer Pudding, 69

tarts

    Treacle Tart, 62

Thick White Sauce, 88

Thin Marmalade, 81

Toad-in-the-Hole, 27–8

Tomato Chutney, Green, 82

tomatoes

    Green Tomato Chutney, 82

    Tomatoes in Vinaigrette
        Dressing, 49–50

Traditional Breakfast Fry, 3

Treacle Tart, 62

vinaigrette dressing, 49–50

White Sauce, Thick, 88

Yorkshire Pudding, 46–7